RNING POINT

The Story of the D-Day Landings

BY MICHAEL BURGAN

Consultant:
Tim Solie
Adjunct Professor of History
Minnesota State University, Mankato, USA

Raintree is an imprint of Capstone Global Library Limited, a company incorporated in England and Wales having its registered office at 264 Banbury Road, Oxford, OX2 7DY – Registered company number: 6695582

www.raintree.co.uk
myorders@raintree.co.uk

Text © Capstone Global Library Limited 2017
The moral rights of the proprietor have been asserted.

Edited by Adrian Vigliano
Designed by Kyle Grenz
Picture research by Tracy Cumm
Production by Laura Manthe
Originated by Capstone Global L
Printed and bound in China.

ISBN 978 1 4747 3272 7 (paperba
21 20 19 18 17
10 9 8 7 6 5 4 3 2 1

British Library Cataloguing in Publication Data
A full catalogue record for this book is available from
the British Library.

Acknowledgements
We would like to thank the following for permission to reproduce photographs:
Alamy: Military Images, 20; Getty Images: Bettmann, 69, Bob Landry/Hulton Archive, 32, David E. Scherman/The LIFE Picture Collection, 45, FPG/Hulton Archive, 26, Popperfoto, 8, 25, 76, 94, Sgt. Wilkes/IWM, 38, ullstein bild, 90, Universal History Archive/UIG, 82; Library of Congress: 19; Naval History & Heritage Command: 43; Newscom: NI Syndication, 14; Shutterstock: Everett Historical, Cover Top, Cover Bottom, 7, 46, 54, 59, 72, 86, Lora liu, Cover Background; Thinkstock: PHOTOS.com, 4, Wikimedia: Archives Normandie 1939-45/National Archives USA, 81, Conseil Régional de Basse-Normandie/National Archives USA, 62

CONTENTS

FOREWORD

With the blast of naval guns and the roar of tanks and planes, Germany invaded Poland on 1 September 1939. This surprise attack marked the start of World War II. Germany, under its dictator, Adolf Hitler, wanted to expand its control over large parts of Europe. As Hitler won more territory, he ordered the killing of millions of people he considered inferior to Germans. Jewish residents of Europe were his top target, but Hitler slaughtered Slavs, Gypsies and others as well.

When the war began, the United States did not join the conflict. Many Americans still remembered the horrors of World War I. They did not want to take part in another war when the United States did not face a direct threat. But after Japan launched a surprise attack on Pearl Harbor, Hawaii, on 7 December 1941, the United States declared war on Japan. That nation and Germany, along with Italy, were allies, and Germany and Italy soon declared war on the United States. US President Franklin D. Roosevelt believed Hitler posed a huge threat to democracy and world peace. "FDR" welcomed the chance to fight Germany as well as Japan.

When the United States entered the war, Germany controlled a large part of Western Europe, including France. The main fighting on the continent was in the east. In June 1941, Germany had invaded the Soviet Union, which stretched from Europe across the northern part of Asia. The United States helped the Soviets by sending supplies, but Soviet leader Joseph Stalin wanted something more. He wanted the United States and Great Britain to open a second front by attacking the Germans in France. That would force Hitler to move troops there from the Eastern Front, where the Soviets battled the Germans.

British prime minister Winston Churchill wanted to attack the Germans in Europe, but he differed with US leaders on where and when the major assault should come. Finally, the Allies agreed to build a huge military force in Great Britain, cross the English Channel in the spring of 1944 and fight the Germans in northwestern France. From there, the plan was to march eastwards, pushing back the German military and destroying its ability to fight. The planned attack was called Operation Overlord. The day picked for the attack was called D-Day.

The USS *Shaw* was destroyed during the attack on Pearl Harbor, when raging fires reached the ship's forward magazine.

WHEN WILL THE ATTACK COME?

1

Dwight D. Eisenhower

Dwight D. Eisenhower

4 June 1944, Southwick, England

General Dwight D. Eisenhower woke early as usual. He and his military advisors met daily at 4.00 a.m. to go over the weather forecast for Normandy, the Allies' target in Operation Overlord. Eisenhower knew that he had only a few days during which he could give the order to begin the Allied landing on the French coast. Only 4–7 June would provide the low tides and full moon his troops needed to begin safely going ashore.

Eisenhower's official title was supreme commander of Allied Expeditionary Forces. Among friends, he was called Ike. He came to London in June 1942 to lead the US troops that would fight in North Africa and Europe. After Allied successes in Africa and Italy, he was chosen to command the Overlord invasion. Eisenhower had never fought on a battlefield, but he had years of experience in training and organizing troops.

Overlord required all his organizational skills, as the Allies amassed ships, planes, tanks and troops for history's largest amphibious invasion. Between the soldiers, sailors, pilots and marines who would do the actual fighting and the military crews that supported them, Eisenhower commanded almost 3 million men. More than half were American, and most of the others came from Great Britain and Canada.

Eisenhower had first hoped to begin the assault on France in May. He knew the Germans were building up their defences along the Normandy coast. Adolf Hitler wanted to build the so-called Atlantic Wall all across Western Europe to try to prevent an Allied invasion. In France, the Germans brought in new artillery and placed mines and obstacles along the beaches. The more time that passed, the stronger the German defences would become. Eisenhower also knew that German scientists were working on new, secret weapons. The Allies needed to prevent the German military from ever using them.

But the supreme commander also wanted to make sure his force was large enough to carry out the invasion as planned. That meant bringing in more equipment. Plus, with extra time, Allied bombers could carry out more attacks on German forces in France, weakening their ability to fight off the invasion. But if the Allies waited too long, they would not have the long days and good weather of summer that would make the fighting easier for them. Out of the four dates in early June that were best for the attack, Eisenhower chose 5 June as D-Day – the departure day for the troops to go ashore in France.

On this day, 4 June, Eisenhower had to consider the role the weather would play in the attack. The 4.00 a.m. meeting to go over the forecast would be his last chance to decide if Overlord would begin the next day. Already, some vessels were at sea, preparing for the first phases of the attack. A storm, however, had settled over Normandy. Eisenhower heard chief meteorologist Captain J.M. Stagg explain the situation. "The clouds will be too thick for the planes to see their targets. And the seas will be rough, tossing around the landing craft supposed to bring the men ashore. It doesn't look good."

Despite the bleak forecast, one of the top commanders under Eisenhower thought the attack should go ahead. Another disagreed, while still another didn't take a strong position either way. The final decision, however, was Eisenhower's alone.

George Honour

Crammed into a space about the size of a bathroom, British naval lieutenant George Honour piloted his mini-submarine towards the Normandy coast. Honour and his crew of four had set sail on the evening of 2 June, staying underwater for hours. Along the way, they passed through German minefields. Now, about 1.5 kilometres offshore, Honour brought the sub just below the water's surface. He raised the vessel's periscope, saying, "Well, gentlemen, let's have a look-see."

Honour had volunteered to do dangerous underwater work two years before. Now he was in charge of a tiny sub called X23. It and another mini-submarine, X20, were supposed to help guide ashore Allied landing craft carrying tanks. They had to be in position before the main invasion, which Honour and his crew knew was supposed to happen the next day. The sailors wore rubber wetsuits, ready to go into the water if the Germans spotted them and attacked. They also carried false identification papers. If they were attacked and could reach land, Honour and his men had to pretend to be local French residents. Their goal – avoid being captured by the Germans and meet up with members of the Resistance,

British sailors used X-Craft mini-submarines to help prepare for the Allied attack on Normandy.

the French citizens who fought against German rule. With help from the Allies, the Resistance gathered intelligence and carried out sabotage against the Germans.

Looking through the periscope, Honour saw German soldiers on the beach near the obstacles meant to slow, if not stop, an Allied invasion. Honour was pleased about one thing. "We're almost bang on the target," he told the crew. X23 was supposed to mark the path for British and Canadian tanks. The specially designed duplex drive (DD) tanks could move both in water and on land. The Allies had named the beach where they were supposed to land Sword.

Satisfied that he had reached the right spot, Honour took the sub down to the bottom of the English Channel. He and his crew would wait for H-Hour – the time when the invasion would begin. Twenty minutes before H-Hour, he and his crew would go to work. But before settling in to wait, he took the sub up one more time so he could get another view of the beach through the periscope. It was Sunday afternoon, and German soldiers were relaxing along the shore and swimming in the water. Honour said, "Little do they know what's in store for them."

As midnight came, X23 came to the surface again, to receive any coded messages sent from England. The radio operator heard, "Your aunt is riding a bicycle today." The men were silent as they prepared to go back underwater. The message meant that General Eisenhower had decided the weather was too bad to attack on 5 June. D-Day would be delayed until the next day. Honour and his men would spend more hours in their tiny sub, eating tinned beans, drinking tea and waiting.

Dwight D. Eisenhower

5 June 1944, Plymouth, England

Delaying the invasion had not been an easy decision to make. Eisenhower and his aides couldn't be sure that the vessels already at sea could return to port and then be ready again to attack on 6 June. Plus, the storm could get worse, and then that perfect time slot for launching Overlord would slip by. That would give the Germans even more time to ready their defences.

Waking up for another 4.00 a.m. weather report, Eisenhower heard fierce winds and pounding rains. He couldn't imagine that Captain Stagg would have good news on the weather. At the meeting, Stagg confirmed that not attacking today had been a wise choice. The weather along the Normandy coast had been as terrible as he expected. But a new forecast suggested that the weather might clear enough on the 6th for the attack to go on. That evening, Eisenhower held a second meeting to discuss the weather and if the Allies should attack. Stagg once again said that the next day looked favourable. Still, the commanders of the Allied air forces worried about the clouds. Once again, the final decision was up to Eisenhower. "I am quite positive we must give the order . . . I don't see how we can do anything else." 6 June 1944 would be D-Day for the invasion of France.

Late that night, Eisenhower recorded a message that the invading forces would hear before they left for France. He said, in part, "I have full confidence in your courage, devotion to duty and skill in battle. We will accept nothing less than full victory!"

General Eisenhower briefs paratroopers in England before they board planes headed to Normandy.

ASSAULT FROM THE AIR

During World War II, both Allied and German forces used gliders to transport troops and equipment.

John Howard

5 June 1944, flying above France

As midnight approached, Major John Howard sat inside a glider plane and thought about what could happen when he and his men reached France. He commanded six gliders, each carrying about 30 highly trained British soldiers. They would be the first Allied troops in France for Operation

Overlord, probably the first to face German fire. Howard wondered: Would a machine gunner spot the gliders as they silently approached land? Would the gliders fly into "Rommel's Asparagus"? Edwin Rommel, the German commander in Normandy, had put up telephone poles that were meant to rip off the wings of incoming gliders. Even without that "asparagus", the landing could be hard, perhaps injuring or even killing some of the men. A hard landing, Howard worried, might also set off the explosives his men carried with them on the planes.

Howard was in Glider #1. The men on board it and two other gliders were supposed to seize a bridge over the Caen Canal. The Allies called it Pegasus Bridge. The men on the other three planes were targeting a bridge over the nearby River Orne. Howard's goal was to capture both bridges so the Germans could not send reinforcements to the beaches where British and Canadian troops were supposed to land. Howard knew the bridges were well guarded. He hoped the element of surprise would let him and his men take the bridges without suffering heavy casualties.

A few kilometres from the target, the bomber planes towing the gliders cut them loose. The gliders descended through the clouds. As they prepared to land, Howard and the other men in his glider linked their arms. Then they raised their feet, in case the floor was smashed during the landing. Howard could see the sweat on the pilot's face as he guided the glider down. The landing knocked Howard's helmet over his eyes, and for a second he could not see. Then he looked out and saw the bridge in the moonlight. Lieutenant Den Brotheridge led the men off the plane. "Come on, lads," he said. He and his men, joined by the soldiers on the other two gliders, quickly took the bridge.

Howard set up his command post near the three gliders. He soon received word that his men in the other three had also captured their target. The mission had taken less than ten minutes. Now Howard's force would have to hold the bridges as the Germans realized what had happened and tried to retake them. Howard's men easily fought off a German patrol. But at 2.00 a.m., Howard saw a much more deadly force approaching his post. Two enemy tanks were only 90 metres away.

Werner Pluskat

6 June 1944, near Bayeux, France

As the sound of gunfire pierced the night's quiet, Major Werner Pluskat, of the German 352nd Infantry Division, woke from his sleep. Pluskat commanded 20 artillery guns along the Normandy beach, though he spent his evenings in a house several kilometres away. Still dazed from sleep, he called artillery headquarters and asked what was going on. "We don't know yet," the officer on the other end said. Pluskat made another call, this one to his unit's intelligence officer. "Probably just another bombing raid, Pluskat," the officer told him.

Pluskat was still awake when he received a phone call at 12.30 a.m. "It seems the invasion is beginning," the voice from headquarters said. Pluskat rounded up two other officers, and along with his German shepherd, Harras, they drove to Pluskat's command post. It was a bunker built into the cliffs that overlooked the beach. Pluskat grew excited because he thought the invasion was finally coming. German commanders had thought the Allies would strike farther north, near the town of Pas-de-Calais. But perhaps Pluskat and his men would see real action too. Taking a pair of binoculars, Pluskat scanned the sea in the moonlight. He saw nothing. Disappointed, he turned to his officers. "Another false alarm."

American paratroopers prepare to
jump into France on D-Day.

HITTING THE GROUND

An estimated 13,100 American paratroopers jumped into France on D-Day.

Dick Winters

6 June 1944,
near Sainte-Mère Église, France

With planes filling the sky, Dick Winters heard
the sound of anti-aircraft fire. Peering through his
plane's open door, he saw red, blue and green streaks
from the tracers the Germans shot at the US planes.

Winters belonged to Company E of the 506th Parachute Infantry Regiment of the 101st Airborne Division. He was the jumpmaster for this flight. His job was to make sure the paratroopers on board the plane had all their equipment and got out of the plane as it came over its target. As the plane neared France, he wondered how he and the others would react when they faced enemy fire.

Winters was part of the next wave of Allied troops to reach France after the gliders landed. More than 20,000 paratroopers would float down at various spots away from the coast. Their mission was to keep German reinforcements away from the beach and make sure the landing forces were not trapped before they could begin to push inland. Winters and his fellow jumpers carried as much as 68 kilograms of equipment. They had to be prepared to survive if they drifted from their target and landed alone behind enemy lines. To communicate with each other, they carried toy "crickets". Pressing down on the metal legs created a noise that sounded like a cricket's chirp.

At about 1.15 a.m., Winters and his stick – the paratroopers on a single plane – neared the town of Sainte-Mère Église. Winters felt energy pulse through his body as he prepared to face combat for the first time. Outside the plane, the German guns seemed to be finding their range. Anti-aircraft fire hit just as Winters yelled "Go!" and made the first jump from the plane. The rest of the stick followed. Winters hit the ground hard. Nearby, he could hear church bells ringing. The fighting would soon begin.

Alexandre Renaud

Alexandre Renaud could feel the ground shake from the Allied bombs falling around his town, Sainte-Mère Église. He was the town pharmacist and also its mayor. He and his family took shelter in their house. They could not find a safer place in town because the Germans had imposed a curfew. Across Normandy, the Germans forced the residents to stay indoors at night.

Someone, though, had risked arrest or being hit by a bomb to come out and knock on the door of Renaud's pharmacy. Renaud went to the door and saw the town's fire chief. He could also see flames from a burning barn near the town's church. "I think it was hit by a stray bullet from one of the planes," the chief said. "The fire is spreading fast."

The chief wanted Renaud to go to the German officer who was in charge in Sainte-Mère Église and ask him to lift the curfew.

"We need as much help as we can get for the bucket brigade," the chief said.

Renaud ran to the building that served as the headquarters for the Germans in the town. He asked the sergeant on duty to lift the curfew, and the sergeant agreed without checking with the commanding officer. Armed German soldiers, though, would go along to watch the citizens as they battled the blaze. Then Renaud went to the church and asked the priest to begin ringing its bell to call the residents to the town centre. Soon about 100 volunteers were passing buckets of water down a line towards the burning barn.

As Renaud and the others fought the fire, the priest came to him and led him inside the church. There, a local woman, obviously upset, told the mayor, "A man has landed in my pea patch." Renaud briefly tried to calm her down before returning to the blaze. He now heard more planes overhead, and soon, he saw men dropping from the sky all around the town. He realized they were paratroopers. Renaud watched as the German soldiers began firing, killing one soldier before he hit the ground. Another landed in a tree and the Germans killed him before he could cut himself free from his parachute. Renaud and the others kept battling the fire as machine guns sprayed bullets through the town centre.

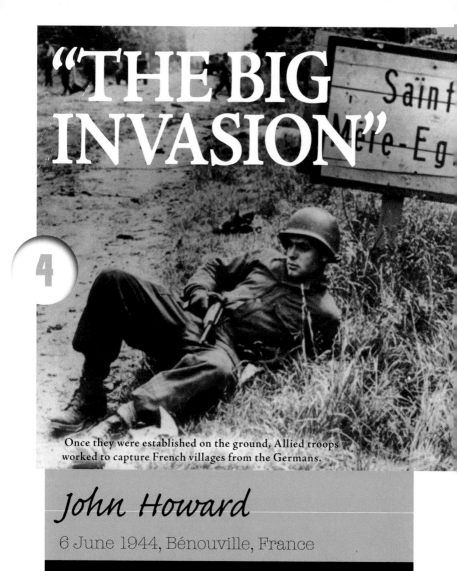

"THE BIG INVASION"

4

Once they were established on the ground, Allied troops worked to capture French villages from the Germans.

John Howard

6 June 1944, Bénouville, France

Major Howard watched the two tanks slowly rolling towards the bridge. Howard asked one of his officers to bring out the only weapon the men

had that could stop a tank. It fired
a bomb about 30 centimetres long.
The job of actually firing it went
to Sergeant Wagger Thornton.
He and another soldier went to
a spot near the bridge, waited
several moments, then fired at the
lead tank. Howard watched with
joy as the anti-tank bomb hit its
intended target. Several German
soldiers jumped out of the damaged
tank and the British soldiers killed
them with their machine guns.
The second tank quickly turned
around. As the morning went on,
British paratroopers landed nearby
to reinforce Howard and his men.
They faced no more major German
challenges as they guarded the
Pegasus Bridge.

Marcelle Hamel-Hateau had gone to bed on the night of 6 June thinking about her boyfriend. The schoolteacher in the village of Neuville-au-Plain had not seen him for four years. He had joined the Free French, the forces who were trying to drive the German occupiers out of France.

As the night went on, Hamel-Hateau and her family heard the sound of planes overhead. They were used to the Allied bombing raids in Normandy, but there were no military targets near their village, so it was unusual for the planes to be so close. The family went outside to investigate, but they didn't see anything. They did hear the hum of more planes nearby.

A little while later, Hamel-Hateau looked out of the window and saw dark shapes falling from the sky. She went outside and spotted a parachute hanging from the roof. Curious and not afraid, she started to walk down the road near her house. She stopped when she saw a man sitting by the road. His body was covered with large bags, and he carried a rifle and a pistol. Hamel-Hateau approached him and asked in English if his plane had been shot down. He said no, then replied in perfect French, "It's the big invasion. . . Thousands and thousands of paratroopers are landing in this countryside tonight."

The paratrooper asked if there were any Germans nearby and Hamel-Hateau said no. He asked if there was somewhere he could look at his map without using a light outside. He didn't want to attraction attention. Hamel-Hateau led the paratrooper into the small classroom where she taught. Her mother, aunt and her neighbours' children joined them. Hamel-Hateau noticed the soldier was limping from a sprained ankle and offered to treat it, but he refused, saying, "I have more important things to worry about now." Spreading out his map, he asked Hamel-Hateau to show him where he had landed. He was shocked to see that he had drifted far from his target. She told him the best route to take to reach the spot where he could meet the other paratroopers from his plane. As he prepared to go, the soldier spoke to her in English so only she could understand him. "The days to come are going to be terrible," he said. "Good luck . . . I will not forget you for the rest of my life." Then Hamel-Hateau watched him slip into the darkness.

Dwight D. Eisenhower
6 June 1944, Southwick, England

When General Eisenhower woke early on the morning of 6 June, he knew the D-Day invasion was underway. He sat in his trailer in the woods and re-read the words he had written. If the invasion did not succeed, he would send out this failure letter to the world:

"Our landings in the Cherbourg-Havre area have failed to gain a satisfactory foothold and I have withdrawn the troops. My decision to attack at this time and place was based upon the best information available. The troops, the air and the Navy did all that bravery and devotion to duty could do. If any blame or fault attaches to the attempt it is mine alone."

Eisenhower put the failure letter in his jacket pocket, then went to another meeting on the weather. Stagg's earlier forecast had been right: the weather looked like it was going to clear a bit. Of course, the weather didn't really matter at this point. The Allies were committed to the attack on Normandy.

"10,000 SHIPS"

An estimated 28,845 British soldiers landed on Sword Beach on D-Day.

Hugh Temple Bone

6 June 1944, the English Channel

For someone with no experience at sea, the water seemed particularly rough to Lieutenant Hugh Temple Bone of the 2nd Battalion, East Yorkshire Regiment. The wind was whipping and the waves swelled as high as 9 metres. Bone's regiment would be part of the first British assault team to come ashore at Sword Beach. It was one of three beaches assigned to British and Canadian forces, along with Juno and Gold.

The regiment had boarded the *Glenearn* and *Empire Battleaxe* the night before at 9.00 p.m. These ships and others like them carried soldiers and the smaller landing craft that would bring them ashore. Bone was a signal officer, meaning he would be collecting and sending messages during the battle. Before leaving England for France, Bone had collected any secret orders the men had and burned them, to make sure the Germans would not find them if any of the men were taken prisoner. Through the night, he wondered if he would ever see his girlfriend or his family again.

Now, nearing the French coast at about 4.30 a.m., the first wave of marines and soldiers entered the landing craft. The men who would follow them cheered them on. Bone had blackened his face so he would be harder to see, and he put on an inflatable vest in case he ended up in the water. Then he waited for the order to go ashore.

Werner Pluskat

6 June 1944, Normandy, France

From his command post, Major Pluskat spent most of the early hours of 6 June scanning the sea. After all the activity earlier in the night, he was surprised he had not received any news from headquarters.

Just after 5.00 a.m., the first rays of sunlight began to shine in the distance. Through the binoculars, Pluskat saw what looked like ships. The longer he looked, the more ships he saw. He couldn't believe how many there were. Pluskat handed the binoculars to one of the other officers and said, "My God, it's the invasion." He picked up the phone to call headquarters. He told the officer who answered that the Allied invasion had begun. "There must be 10,000 ships out there." The officer dismissed the idea, saying,

"The Americans and British together don't have that many ships. Nobody has that many ships!"

The officer then asked which way the ships were heading. Pluskat replied, "Right for me."

Joseph Dawson

The choppy seas had made it hard for the men in Captain Joseph Dawson's regiment to board their landing craft. Most had to climb down nets cast over the side of the *Henrico*, the ship that carried them from England to France. Dawson commanded Company G of the 16th Infantry Regiment, part of the US Army's 1st Infantry Division. The division's nickname was "the Big Red One". Its members had fought during World War I and Dawson's company had already seen action in Italy.

By 4.45 a.m. Dawson and his men were in their landing craft and moving towards shore. During the trip to the Normandy coast, they could hear the huge guns from British and US warships firing at the German defences. Company G was heading for the beach the Allies had named Omaha. General Eisenhower and his aides knew the Germans had their strongest defences at this beach. Their artillery were set up high on cliffs above the shore, and they had also built defensive structures closer to the water. The shelling from the naval ships and bombing from US planes were supposed to weaken the German defences before Dawson's company came ashore. Soldiers in the landing craft cheered as they watched the bombers head for their targets.

American troops in a LCVP landing craft approach Omaha Beach on D-Day.

H-Hour for Company G was 7.00 a.m., just after the first wave of Americans hit Omaha Beach. Before any of the infantry came ashore, demolition teams would destroy the obstacles the Germans had placed in the water, and then tanks would go through the openings. Before that, though, Dawson and the others in the Big Red One faced a bumpy ride. Sea spray soaked the men, and many hung over the side of their vessels, throwing up the breakfast they had eaten several hours before.

Rough seas on D-Day made seasickness a widespread problem among invading troops.

COMING
ASHORE

6

Werner Pluskat

The enemy ships continued to fire on shore while their landing craft moved closer. Major Pluskat was inside his bunker in the cliff overlooking the beach. The shells shook the bunker and sent him to the ground. Dust from the concrete filled the air, and his binoculars were smashed. As the shelling continued, the phone rang. Someone at headquarters wanted to know the exact location of the shelling. "They're falling all over," Pluskat screamed into the phone. "What do you want me to do – go out and measure the holes with a ruler?"

During a break in the shelling, Pluskat contacted all the crews manning his largest guns. The shelling and Allied bombs had not damaged any of them. Pluskat passed that good news along to headquarters. He then reminded the gun crews not to fire too soon. He said, "No guns must fire until the enemy reaches the water's edge."

Heinrich Severloh

6 June 1944,
near Colleville-sur-Mer, France

For several hours, German Corporal Heinrich Severloh had sat in a concrete bunker above some sand dunes, a machine gun by his side. Barbed wire and mines guarded the entrance to the bunker. Severloh was positioned in Widerstandnest ["resistance nest"] 62. The nest was a series of bunkers connected by trenches, with ceilings nearly 2 metres thick. Along with Severloh, 19 other men operated guns of different sizes. Resistance nests like these were built all along this stretch of the Normandy coast, and gunners like Severloh were supposed to shoot incoming Allied troops that came ashore.

Only 20 years old, Severloh had been a farmer before the war. He had served on the Eastern Front before being sent to France. Severloh's nest guarded a German observation post. Soldiers there would give the location of incoming enemy ships to large artillery batteries several kilometres away from the beach. Severloh and the others with him were part of Major Werner Pluskat's artillery of the 352nd Infantry Division.

As daylight approached, Severloh saw an eerie sight in the distance – ships, a lot of them, of all sizes. As they approached the shore, Severloh heard the sound of aeroplanes drawing closer.

"Bombers!" Severloh's sergeant called out. Anyone not inside the bunker quickly took cover. A bomb from an enemy plane landed about 45 metres from the nest. Its blast shook the concrete bunker and sent dirt flying, but no one was hurt. The bombers passed overhead, but then Severloh heard the sound of incoming shells. Allied warships were beginning to bombard the shore. Once again the ground shook as more and more shells landed near the bunker. The smoke from the exploding shells darkened the sky. Finally, the firing stopped.

No one in Widerstandnest 62 died from this first attack, though Severloh and several others were slightly wounded. "It's just a bump," the corporal said, feeling where a piece of a shell had bounced off his head. He and the others returned to their guns and saw small landing craft heading towards the shore. "They're coming!" someone shouted. Severloh assumed they were British soldiers, until he saw the letters "US" painted on one of the boats.

Ken Reynolds

Bullets and shells flew all around Seaman Second Class Ken Reynolds even before his landing craft reached the shore. As a member of the Naval Combat Demolition Unit (NCDU), Reynolds was one of 175 seamen now entering the water just off Omaha Beach. They were trained to blow up the metal obstacles that blocked access to the beach. Along with US Army engineers, they were supposed to clear 16 paths 15 metres wide, so more landing craft could reach the shore. While Reynolds and others worked at Omaha Beach, NCDU teams and Army engineers were carrying out the same task at Utah Beach, the other target for US forces.

It was about 6.30 a.m. when Reynolds and the others jumped from the landing craft into shallow water to make the last push towards the obstacles. He and five other men pulled a small rubber raft filled with explosives. As the German fire grew heavier, the men grabbed all the explosives they could from the raft and let it go. Reynolds thought to himself,

"Blow the obstacles. Do the job. Don't get killed. Get to the beach."

Allied bombers were supposed to have knocked out the German defences, but it was clear they had not done the job.

Reynolds was just 18, and the only weapon he carried was a knife. He watched as direct hits destroyed several boats nearby, surely killing most of the NCDU members on board. He tried to ignore the dead bodies in the water around him and continue with his mission. He carried 32 small explosives that he was going to attach to the different obstacles. He had trained to blow up huge steel frames called Belgian Gates that formed a wall off the coast. Reynolds also destroyed mines set up on posts and obstacles called hedgehogs, which had crossed steel beams 1.5 metres tall. All the time he worked, the Germans kept firing and killing many of the other demolition experts.

While the NCDU teams set their explosives, some infantry began to reach the shore in their landing craft. Leaving the boats, they took cover behind some of the obstacles still in the water – obstacles the sailors had just rigged to explode.

ON THE BEACHES

7

An estimated 34,250 American soldiers landed
on Omaha Beach on D-Day.

Ken Reynolds

"Get out of there! Get out!" Over the sounds of battle, Reynolds yelled at the soldiers taking cover by the obstacle. In two minutes, the obstacle would blow up.

Instead of listening to Reynolds' warning and moving on, more frightened soldiers took cover behind the obstacle. Reynolds kept yelling and went over and began pulling soldiers away before the obstacle exploded. Now, with the enemy fire increasing, Reynolds and the other NCDU members near him made their way towards the beach, hoping to find their own safe spot. On the shore, he looked back towards the water and saw that his team had cleared a lane through the obstacles. It was wide enough for two landing craft to pass through at the same time. Because of the heavy enemy shelling, the NCDU and the Army engineers could not open as many lanes as their commanders had hoped. But there were enough passages for thousands of men to come ashore on Omaha Beach in the first hours of the invasion.

Hugh Temple Bone
6 June 1944, off Sword Beach, France

The ride on the landing craft to Sword Beach was wet and bumpy. H-Hour for the 2nd Battalion was 7.25 a.m., and they seemed to be right on target. Normally Lieutenant Bone hated chewing gum, but now he chewed a piece. When H-Hour came, he turned on his radio and began receiving reports from the men already battling on the shore: "Heavy opposition, pushing on." "Heavy casualties, pushing on." Bone heard the sounds of warfare too – the rat-a-tat of German machine gun fire and the explosions of their mortars.

Approaching the shore, the landing craft bumped into an obstacle with a mine on top of it. "Just like in the photos they showed us," Bone thought. Luckily, the craft didn't hit the mine head on and set it off.

Both enemy and Allied artillery exploded all around the vessel, which finally reached the beach.

As the doors opened to let out the members of the 2nd Battalion, Bone saw some of the soldiers around him fall into the water. Bone concentrated on keeping dry the radio set he would need to carry out his duties. He and some other men got the radio ashore and then began digging holes they could use for protection. Without looking up, Bone could tell that German bullets were hitting some of the British troops around him.

Bone moved off the beach but then received an order to go back to the boats to round up men who had not made it far ashore, and to get more radio gear. Despite the battle raging around him, Bone was not afraid – he was focused on doing his job. But he couldn't totally ignore the bloody bodies of dead soldiers and the cries for help from the wounded. Some of the casualties included members of his own radio team, whom he found taking cover behind a damaged tank. Further on, he saw some wounded soldiers who could still walk. Bone convinced them to help carry the radio sets still on the shore.

Joseph Dawson

At 7.00 a.m., Captain Dawson was the first man off his landing craft. Only two others followed him off before a German shell hit the vessel, destroying it with the rest of the men still on board. Among the 30 dead Dawson counted was a naval officer who was supposed to tell the US warships offshore where to fire. Now Dawson couldn't count on any help from their big guns. Heading ashore, he could hear the whizzing sound of German bullets that missed their targets and the thuds of the ones that hit US soldiers around him. He saw dead bodies covering the beach.

A group of soldiers from Company G who had already landed tried to take cover behind a pile of small rocks called a shingle. The beach at Omaha was more like gravel than sand, and the water had pushed some of it into a mound. Dawson organized the men there and tried to work out a way to advance. "Follow me," he shouted at three men who were lying behind the shingle, not moving. Maybe they didn't hear him over the raging battle, or maybe they were simply too scared to move. After a moment, Dawson realized they were dead.

Staying on the beach, Dawson realized, meant certain death. But on the other side of the shingle, the Germans had set up barbed wire and a minefield. Dawson had two of his men set off an explosive to cut a hole in the wire fence, and then the men carefully worked their way through the minefield.

American soldiers exit their landing craft to attack Omaha Beach on D-Day.

He and his men made their way up a hill in the direction of some of the German gunners. Along the way, they came upon about 20 men from Company E. So far, they were the only other soldiers from the Big Red One whom Dawson had seen make it off the beach.

Carefully moving upwards, Dawson heard German machine gun fire and soldiers speaking German. He was able to move up undetected and throw two grenades into the Germans' position. The gun fell silent, and now the Americans could more easily move forwards.

Heinrich Severloh
6 June 1944,
near Colleville-sur-Mer, France

Corporal Severloh watched the Americans leave their landing craft and jump into water up to their chests. He and the other men in the bunker called the Americans Amis. The name was something of a joke, as in French the word meant "friends".

The men in the resistance nest had orders not to fire until the enemy was closer to the shore. When that moment came, all the guns in the bunker exploded into action. Severloh pulled the trigger on his machine gun and watched the spray his bullets made as they hit the water. The Americans, struggling under the weight of their heavy packs, dived into the water. Some died from the German fire while others drowned in the shallow water. As more landing craft came towards the shore, Severloh fired at the men as soon as they stepped out. He saw Americans dive for cover behind the obstacles General Rommel's men had placed in the water. Other Americans tried to hide behind the men killed just moments before. The constant firing of Severloh's machine gun caused it to overheat. He then picked up his rifle and fired with that, letting the larger gun cool down before he loaded his next rounds.

IN THE VILLAGES

8

Allied troops had to move through French villages carefully, watching out for hidden German snipers and other hazards.

As dawn came, more American paratroopers passed through the village of Neuville-au-Plain and approached the Hamel-Hateau house. One group knocked, looking for German soldiers. Another stopped by the schoolhouse and, seeing the teacher, a soldier motioned for her to come over. He pointed to a spot on the map he needed to reach.

"We don't want to use the main roads," the soldier explained. "We want to avoid the Germans."

"Yes, you can get there along the back roads," Hamel-Hateau said. "But the directions are complicated. Let me take you there."

"No, we can't let you do that. It's too dangerous," said the soldier.

"Do you have another choice?" asked Hamel-Hateau.

The soldier finally agreed, and he and the others set off with Hamel-Hateau. As they walked, gunfire erupted near them. The soldiers stopped, and their guide felt her heart jump into her throat. But they continued on, running along some hedges that provided some cover. Finally, Hamel-Hateau led them to the road that would take them to their destination. She returned home alone, with the walk seeming to take forever.

Dick Winters

6 June 1944, Normandy, France

By 7.00 a.m., Winters and his men were in a tiny village about 2.5 kilometres away from Sainte Marie-du-Mont. He had orders to take out four German artillery guns not far away. US intelligence had not spotted them before because they were well hidden in trenches. The guns had just started firing on the American troops coming ashore at Utah Beach.

Winters' company had two light machine guns, and he positioned them so they could provide cover for the men who would approach the German guns. They would get as close as they could and then throw grenades into trenches. As he crawled forwards towards the target, Winters noticed the head of a German soldier peeking up above a trench. He aimed his rifle and fired two shots. The German fell over, dead.

Winters and his men reached the first artillery gun and threw their grenades, and the Germans fired rifles and threw their own grenades. Private "Popeye" Wynn was hit, and rather than cry out in pain, he said to Winters, "I'm sorry, Lieutenant, I goofed. I goofed. I'm sorry." Winters was impressed that the private was more concerned about letting down the other soldiers in his company than with his injury.

Winters and his men killed the Germans nearby and moved on to the second gun. Rushing it with guns blaring, yelling as they ran, Winters and his men soon captured the second gun. Reinforcements arrived and they all moved on to the third gun, taking it and capturing six prisoners. The Germans had approached them with their hands over their heads, saying in poor English, "No make me dead!" Men from Company D had now joined Company E and they led the assault on the final gun.

Their mission accomplished, Winters and his men began to pull back, as Germans in the distance were still firing on them. By now, it was mid-morning. Winters and his men took satisfaction in knowing they had defeated a larger German force, and probably saved the lives of soldiers still pouring onto Utah Beach.

Theodore Roosevelt Jr

6 June 1944, Utah Beach, France

When the first wave of American troops reached Utah Beach, General Theodore Roosevelt Jr was with them. At 56, he was the oldest man in the invasion force, and he was the only American general to come ashore in the first wave. Roosevelt was the oldest son of former US president Theodore Roosevelt and a cousin of current president Franklin Roosevelt. The general's father had led a famous charge up San Juan Hill in Cuba during the Spanish-American War of 1898. Roosevelt Jr had fought bravely during World War I, taking a German bullet to the leg. The wound and arthritis forced him to walk with a cane. But even with that old injury and heart problems, Roosevelt insisted on returning to battle after the United States entered World War II.

He had also insisted on being with his men of the 4th Infantry Division when they stormed Utah Beach on D-Day. Before the attack, when Roosevelt made this request, his commander, General Raymond Barton, turned him down. Roosevelt, though, refused to give up. He wrote in a note to Barton, "It will steady the boys to know I am with them."

Roosevelt's men began leaving their landing craft at 6.30 a.m. The general hated military helmets, so he wore a cloth cap instead. Coming ashore with German shells flying through the air, Roosevelt was calm. He had his cane in one hand and a pistol in the other. But he sensed something was wrong. The landmarks in front of him on the beach were not the same as the ones he and the other officers had studied before the assault. Walking to nearby dunes, Roosevelt scanned the landscape. He realized that, somehow, he and his men had landed far from where they were supposed to. More men and tanks were coming ashore. Having landed in the wrong spot, they might be confused about what to do. But Roosevelt couldn't risk trying to get them to their original landing spot under heavy German fire.

The general turned to a colonel nearby. "We have landed in the wrong spot," Roosevelt said, "but we will start the war from here." Roosevelt's radio wasn't working, so he had to walk along the beach to give orders. He directed men and tanks as they came ashore as the shells exploded all around him.

Theodore Roosevelt Jr

Werner Pluskat

6 June 1944, Normandy, France

As the invasion went on and his artillery guns blasted the shore, Major Pluskat tried to make his way back to division headquarters. He drove in his kubelwagen (bucket wagon), the German version of a jeep. A US shell, however, hit the vehicle. Pluskat somehow survived, but the vehicle was destroyed. Continuing on foot, he ran down the road, but enemy fighter planes overhead strafed him and any other Germans who moved. Pluskat threw himself into a ditch, his clothes torn and blood running down his face.

Before reaching the ditch, he had seen dozens of dead Germans, killed either by the bombardment from the ships offshore or the planes that kept zooming above the French countryside. Now, trying to move on, Pluskat crawled down the road. Ahead of him, he saw a farmhouse. As he got closer, he hoped to ask whoever lived there for a glass of water. Through an open door, he saw two Frenchwomen sitting inside. They saw the bloodied German officer and one laughed at him and said in French, "It's terrible, isn't it." She meant the Allied attack, and Pluskat knew she was joking. For four years, the French had watched German forces arrest them and control their lives. Pluskat knew they had no sympathy for the Germans. He did not ask for any water. He just kept crawling.

THE BATTLES CONTINUE

9

The troops advancing through Normandy relied on support from the air to help them clear German positions and guns.

Hugh Temple Bone

6 June 1944, Normandy, France

As the fighting went on, the 2nd Battalion moved off the beach. Bone and the men around him waded through a muddy marsh, the water up to their armpits, as mortars fell all around them.

They rested for a while as other soldiers moved forward to fight the Germans, finally taking control of an enemy position near some woods. From there, Bone watched as his fellow soldiers launched an assault on a larger German position. The Germans, though, were firing mortars, and Bone watched as men around him died in the explosions. With bombs bursting all around him, Bone could not run. And the ground was too hard for him to dig a foxhole that might provide some cover.

Lying face down, Bone saw a sergeant near him take some shrapnel. Bone crawled over to try to help him. He saw that the sergeant had been wounded in the back and neck.

"Easy now," Bone said, treating the neck wound. "You'll be all right." Meanwhile, the fighting went on all around them.

Joseph Dawson
6 June 1944, Colleville-sur-Mer, France

By knocking out the German guns, Captain Dawson and his men had made it easier for more Americans to stream up the hill. Dawson now led Company G to its main goal, the village of Colleville-sur-Mer. Drawing closer to the town, he saw a German soldier in the steeple of the church. He must have seen the Americans, as they soon came under German fire.

Dawson and two of his men advanced on the church and killed its defenders, though one of the Americans was killed in the battle. Leaving the church, Dawson heard gunfire. A German sniper was taking aim at him. The sniper's first bullet missed, but the next struck the wooden stock of Dawson's gun.

The pieces of the shattered wood lodged in Dawson's knee and leg. After a flash of fear, he regained his senses, ignored the pain and regrouped with his men.

In the afternoon, Dawson's company came under attack from Germans hiding in some of the village's stone houses. As the fighting went on, shells began to fall on the village. Dawson realized that the US Navy was firing on Colleville, not knowing he and his men were there. Dawson had lost his radio operator and couldn't send word that US troops were there. He could only watch with shock and anger as the US shells killed more of his men than the Germans did.

SURVEYING THE SCENE

Allied tanks make their way through a devastated French town.

Theodore Roosevelt Jr

6 June 1944, Utah Beach, France

The German opposition at Utah Beach was not too heavy, and General Roosevelt stood on the shore, smoking a pipe and directing the incoming traffic of jeeps, trucks and tanks. To one general reaching the scene he called out, "Keep right on the road, you're doing fine!" German shells, though, still hit American targets. If one damaged a truck and it blocked the road, tanks quickly pushed it out of the way. Roosevelt was determined to get the US forces onto and then off the beach as quickly as possible, before the Germans could launch a counter-attack.

After a few hours, Roosevelt's commander arrived on the beach.

General Barton and Roosevelt saw each other and exchanged a warm greeting. "When I said you could go in the first wave," Barton said, "I never thought I'd see you alive again."

"I'm alive, all right!" Roosevelt said. "Come on, there's work to do. Help me direct traffic."

The two generals kept the vehicles moving, and when Barton learned another spot on the beach was clear, he sent tanks to meet up with the men coming ashore there. Despite the error in landing off their target, the Americans at Utah Beach were making good progress.

Heinrich Severloh

6 June 1944,
near Colleville-sur-Mer, France

The enemy had been storming the beach for three hours when Corporal Severloh had a chance to stop firing and survey the scene. He saw hundreds of dead Americans on the beach, with the rising tide continuing to wash more bodies ashore. Meanwhile, the wounded struggled to find cover.

But even with the killing Severloh and his fellow gunners had done, the Americans kept coming. Landing craft continued to hit the beach, and ships offshore fired at the German nests and bunkers. Severloh ran out of normal ammunition for his machine gun and began firing tracers. The colourful streaks they created in the air made it easier for enemy gunners to find his bunker. Shells from offshore began to land closer and closer.

"It's time to go," the sergeant with Severloh said. "Up the cliffs. If we're lucky, we'll reach headquarters."

Outside the bunker, holes from the largest American shells provided some cover. Severloh darted from one hole to another as he made his way to the nearest road. After going down the road a bit, he waited to see if the other soldiers from his nest were safe. Only one man, dazed from the battle, came up to him. "The others are all dead," the man said. Together, he and Severloh made it to headquarters. There, a commander said, "We're waiting for the tanks. Then we'll kick those Americans out again."

Dwight D. Eisenhower
6 June 1944, near Southwick, England

Through the morning, reports reached Eisenhower on the Allies' progress. He learned first that the air invasion had gone well. At 8.00 a.m. he had reported to US officials, "All preliminary reports are satisfactory. Airborne formations apparently landed in good order . . . Preliminary bombings by air went off as scheduled." Later he learned that his men had come ashore on all five beaches.

He would not need the note in his pocket announcing failure. Instead, at 9.33 a.m., an aide sent out the message that the invasion of Normandy was underway. At 10.00 a.m., the BBC played a message Eisenhower had recorded earlier. The BBC broadcast in many languages around the world, and Eisenhower's message was meant to give hope to the people who were suffering under German rule. He said, "Although the initial assault may not have been made in your own country, the hour of your liberation is approaching."

Allied troops gather German prisoners at a temporary command post on Omaha Beach.

SURROUNDED

Two German child soldiers, captured by the Allies

Werner Pluskat

Wounded and dazed, Major Pluskat managed to get back to his headquarters at 1.00 p.m. The officers there gave him a drink, and Pluskat brought it to his mouth with shaking hands. His men informed him that the batteries were running out of ammunition. Pluskat called his commanders, who were far from the fighting, and shouted into the phone, "When will it arrive? You people don't seem to realize what it's like up here."

The colonel on the other end said the ammunition was on its way. But just 10 minutes later, the colonel called back Pluskat.

"I've got bad news," the colonel said.

"The Americans have destroyed the trucks that were bringing the ammo. It will be nightfall before anything gets up to you."

Pluskat was not surprised. He knew how dangerous the roads were. He also knew his men were likely to run out of ammunition before evening.

Marcelle Hamel-Hateau

6 June 1944, Neuville-au-Plain, France

After guiding the Americans to the road, Marcelle Hamel-Hateau safely returned to her village. She saw the residents welcoming more US paratroopers. But the Germans were still in the area, and as the afternoon went on, Hamel-Hateau heard bullets. She cautiously went down a road and came upon a US soldier in some bushes. She almost spoke to him until he signalled her to be quiet. Then he motioned down the road, where Hamel-Hateau saw some German soldiers marching in single file. She headed off in the other direction, back towards her home. Once inside, she heard the firing of a machine gun nearby rattling the windows. The joy she had felt in the morning when she realized the Americans had landed was now gone. How long would it take for the Germans to leave for good?

Heinrich Severloh

6 June 1944,
near Colleville-sur-Mer, France

From the field headquarters, Severloh and some others headed towards Colleville-sur-Mer, hoping to find more Germans who had survived the American invasion. As night fell, enemy machine fire burst around them, and Severloh jumped into a ditch for cover. He considered his situation: *We are a small, lost group,* he thought, *with few weapons and few prospects, surrounded by enemies. . .* Severloh knew he had fought bravely, but now he realized that for him the war was over. A small tear rolled down his face, unseen in the night's darkness.

DAY'S END

12

Dick Winters

6 June 1944, Normandy, France

With the German guns knocked out, more US troops came towards Winters and his men. They were soon followed by tanks. Winters climbed aboard one tank. He wanted to make sure any Germans hiding in the hedges across a nearby road didn't stay there for long. "I want fire . . . over there, and there, and there . . . clean out anything that's left." With their cannons and machine guns, the tanks followed Winters' orders. Soon, the area was completely under American control.

The Germans had hidden their guns near a house called Brecourt Manor. With the fighting over, the French family who lived there came out and excitedly greeted the Americans.

The father, Winters learned, had fought the Germans during World War I, and the family had lost two sons during the German invasion of France in 1940.

Moving on, Winters and his men found the field headquarters for their division commander. Company E would spend the night of 6 June just outside the village of Culoville. Before going to bed, Winters went out for one last patrol. He heard the sound of footsteps on a cobblestone street and knew they were Germans. Their boots had nails in the bottom that clacked on the stones. Judging that he was outnumbered, Winters leapt into a ditch by the road. The soldiers were so close when they passed that he could smell tobacco on their clothes. The Germans moved on, and Winters returned safely to camp.

Before going to sleep after his long day, Winters said a prayer:

"Thank you, God, for helping me to live through this day, and please help me again tomorrow."

Kurt Meyer

By 7.00 a.m., General Kurt Meyer knew his men would be heading into battle, he just didn't know when. Meyer was in charge of the 12th SS Panzer Division. Panzers were German tanks that had caused so much destruction during the early years of the war, helping Germany achieve its first victories. Meyer belonged to the Waffen (Armed) SS, which had developed out of the private security force Adolf Hitler had created for his Nazi Party. The SS were the most loyal of Germany's fighters and its members considered themselves an elite force. Meyer had already fought across Europe and earned several medals for his bravery.

With the Normandy invasion, however, the panzer divisions faced confusion. Meyer's was called the Hitlerjugend, or Hitler Youth. Its members were only 17 or 18 years old, but they had volunteered to go through rigorous training because of their love of Hitler and Germany. Although the Hitlerjugend had never faced enemy fire, Meyer was convinced they were ready to fight. But his panzer division was one of several under

Kurt Meyer

Hitler's direct command. Only he could give the word for the 12th to enter combat. Finally, just before 4.00 p.m., Meyer received the word to prepare his men. They would head northwest, towards the invading enemy forces. Meyer saw confidence in the eyes of his young soldiers. But he and the other experienced officers knew they faced a rough fight.

As the division rolled along towards the city of Caen, enemy planes roared overhead, strafing the Germans on the ground. Meyer saw woods along the road that would have offered his division some protection, but they had to keep moving towards the front. Meyer saw a soldier hit by enemy fire. Blood gushed from his throat, but there was no time to stop and try to help him.

That night, Meyer went ahead of his men and entered Caen. He saw the destruction from the US and British bombers. Fires burned throughout the city, and buildings had been reduced to rubble. Meyer and his men would try to keep the advancing enemy troops out of the city. But that battle would come tomorrow.

Through the day on 6 June General Eisenhower visited other generals and continued to gather reports from the field. He met with General Bernard "Monty" Montgomery in his cabin, which had photos of enemy generals on the walls. Monty said the pictures helped him to understand the Germans better. The British general had worked closely with Eisenhower in planning D-Day and was the commander of the ground forces still pouring ashore in Normandy. Eisenhower offered to let Montgomery meet with reporters and discuss the invasion – as much as the Allies could discuss an ongoing attack.

Eisenhower also met with Lieutenant General Frederick Morgan. This British officer had helped plan the Overlord invasion even before Eisenhower became involved.

Eisenhower reminded Morgan of all the hard work he had done to make the invasion happen. "Well, you finished it," Morgan replied.

By the evening, Eisenhower had a good sense of what the Allies had accomplished. More then 150,000 men were now ashore on the five target beaches. Some troops had been able to advance inland, but the Americans had not gained much ground at Omaha Beach. He learned about the men who had missed their targets, such as at Utah Beach, and that the Germans had more men at Omaha than his intelligence had predicted. He also saw that Caen was not under Allied control, as General Montgomery had hoped it would be. The different landing forces were also still far from one another. They needed to unite to march forwards against the German counter-attack still to come. Tomorrow, Eisenhower would go ashore at Omaha and see for himself the challenges the Allies still faced.

D-DAY
PLUS ONE

Like many French villages, the town of Caen suffered terrible damage
during the Normandy invasion.

General Meyer had not slept during his night in Caen. In the morning, he talked on the phone to his commander. The general wanted Meyer to join with another panzer division and "throw the enemy into the sea". Meyer then headed back to his division. He saw again the destruction the US and British bombs had caused in the city. *Where is the Luftwaffe,* he wondered? The German air force seemed to have played only a small role in the first day of the invasion.

Meyer assembled his men and they began to move north. With no German planes challenging them, the US and British planes once again strafed any Germans on the road. That included Meyer and the driver of his kubelwagen. Time and again, they had to stop and take cover. Behind them, Meyer's panzers rumbled along. Meyer finally reached a monastery outside Caen. From a church tower, he could see the enemy ships off the coast and their tanks moving in the distance. Then he spotted tanks closer to the monastery. "Do not fire!" he ordered. "Fire only on my command." The enemy tank commander did not realize that panzers were waiting for him. Meyer wanted the enemy to be in just the right position before his men opened fire.

Joseph Dawson
7 June 1944, Normandy, France

The wound in Captain Dawson's leg bothered him through the night of 6 June. His knee was swollen and painful. Now, he prepared to return to England. But he knew the injury was not serious, and hoped that he would soon be back with his men in France, fighting the Germans.

Heinrich Severloh

7 June 1944,
near Colleville-sur-Mer, France

As the sun rose, Severloh and the other men who had spent the night in the ditch climbed out. They made their way through bushes and entered a field. Standing in front of them stood 30 Amis, pointing their guns. Severloh knew his fighting days were over. He would surely spend the rest of the war as a prisoner.

Dick Winters

7 June 1944, Normandy, France

To Lieutenant Winters and the other Americans on the ground in France, it was now D+1. Yesterday's fighting had been hard, but there was more to come. That morning, Winters received orders for Company E to lead their battalion in the advance towards the town of Vierville. As they marched, they came under enemy fire. The battalion wiped out the enemy and took about 140 prisoners. Company E kept going, and with the help of two tanks took the village of Angoville. Winters and his men fought through the day and into the night. They were tired, after getting little sleep since getting the order on 5 June to prepare for D-Day. But they were ready to keep moving through France.

Kurt Meyer

7 June 1944, Normandy, France

As the lead enemy tank crossed the road, Meyer gave the signal for his men to open fire. The tank was soon on fire from a German shell, and the crew scrambled to escape. Soon more enemy tanks were ablaze. The panzers quickly won the battle, and Meyer's men began rounding up prisoners. He saw for the first time that they were fighting Canadians.

Taking a motorcycle, Meyer rode out to watch another division of panzers still engaged in battle. As he rode in the open, Canadian tank shells began to fall around him. Finally, an explosion near him threw Meyer from his motorcycle. As smoke from the exploding shells filled the air, Meyer found himself in a bomb crater – next to a Canadian soldier. The two enemies eyed each other closely, but soon their attention turned to the artillery and naval shells falling around them. Meyer's motorcycle was destroyed. He also saw German tanks not far away. He climbed out and ran towards them, while the Canadian ran in the other direction. Meyer made it to the tanks, and the fighting continued, as Meyer and his men tried to stop the advancing Canadians.

Dwight D. Eisenhower

7 June 1944, the English Channel

The morning after D-Day, General Eisenhower travelled to Portsmouth and boarded the *Apollo*. The British ship was normally used to lay mines, but today it took the supreme commander and several US and British officers to Normandy. The *Apollo* travelled through a lane that had been cleared of German mines, and more ships were looking for remaining mines. The *Apollo* finally reached Omaha Beach, and General Omar Bradley and his aide boarded the ship, along with several naval officers. Bradley was in charge of the 1st US Army Group, though for now those men were under the command of General Montgomery. Once the Allies had total control of the landing areas, Bradley would take control of the group.

From Bradley and his aide, Eisenhower learned more about the fierce fighting that had taken place at Omaha. The Americans were not able to move off the beach until 3.30 p.m., after facing stiff resistance from the Germans' 352nd Infantry Division. Now, though, the Americans were several kilometres inland, and more men and supplies were landing on the shore.

Eisenhower visited the British beaches as well and heard that things were going smoothly. The general never left the *Apollo*, as he welcomed the officers who had been on the battlefield onto his ship. During the various meetings, Eisenhower and his men heard Allied planes continuing their bombing missions, while naval ships fired at targets far from the shore. During the day and into the evening, Eisenhower heard four alerts that indicated German aircraft might be nearby. But none ever got close to the ship. The most challenging moment of the day came when the *Apollo* ran aground on a sand bar and Eisenhower and the other officers were forced to switch to another ship. Finally, around 10.00 p.m., Eisenhower returned to Portsmouth. He would have more important decisions to make the next day, and over the next weeks, as the Allies continued their assault on the Germans.

EPILOGUE

The successful invasion of Normandy on D-Day, 6 June 1944, came at a high cost. The Allies had more than 10,000 casualties, though some of the men first reported missing in action were later found alive. Still, the number could have been higher if the Allies had not been able to deceive the Germans. Hitler and his commanders believed the major Allied invasion of France would come farther to the north, at Pas-de Calais. The Germans also thought Eisenhower had an even larger force than the one he had assembled to storm the Normandy beaches. Even after D-Day, Eisenhower kept having his staff send out false messages to try to trick the Germans. The messages hinted that a larger second invasion could still happen to the north. Hitler waited until 8 June to send reserve troops stationed in the east to fight the Allies in Normandy. Then, as more false messages suggested the Allies would invade again, Hitler cancelled the order.

The Allies also had some luck on their side on 6 June. General Edwin Rommel, the commander of the German defences in Normandy, was in Germany when the attack came. A skilled general, he could not personally direct the German response in the first day of the attack. The Germans also hesitated in sending tanks to the front, allowing the Allies more time to come ashore and move inland.

Despite the success of D-Day, the Allies needed almost a week to close the gaps between the five beaches and then begin their breakout – the effort to capture more territory from the Germans and push them out of France. To keep men and supplies coming ashore, the Allies built portable harbours called mulberries. They sat just off the beaches and let supply boats bring in equipment from larger ships in the English Channel. The Allies needed to keep throwing more men and tanks at the Germans, who were beginning to launch a counter-attack. It took until 27 June for the Americans to capture the port of Cherbourg.

Meanwhile, the British and Canadians struggled to push the Germans out of Caen. In one of the atrocities of the war, German soldiers under the command of Kurt Meyer killed more than 20 Canadians they had taken prisoner.

The fighting in northern France went on through the summer. Helping the Allies was the French Resistance. They blew up railways and bridges to delay the arrival of German reinforcements. On 15 August, the Allies launched a second invasion. This one came in the south, along the Mediterranean coast. In Operation Dragoon, the Allies faced much less resistance as they came ashore. They then worked their way north, to link up with the forces that had landed in Normandy. For the French, a highlight of the war came on 25 August, when the city of Paris was finally freed from German control.

As the Allies pushed east, the Germans launched a last major offensive in December. Fighting in the forests of Belgium, this came to be called the Battle of the Bulge. The Germans advanced far enough west to create a bulge in the Allies' line of troops. But in the end, the German offensive failed, and the Allies resumed their march towards and then into Germany. Meanwhile, Soviet troops were advancing westwards. Caught between the enemy on two sides, Germany finally surrendered. Eisenhower sent a brief message to Washington D.C. in the United States: "The mission of this Allied Force was fulfilled at 0241 local time, 7 May 1945."

That victory would not have come if D-Day had failed. But skill and bravery, along with some luck, won the day for the Allies on 6 June. Today, the memories of that day and the men who fought are preserved in cemeteries across Normandy and in museums in different countries. The first day of any important mission can be called a D-Day. But the world remembers one D-Day in particular, the Allies' first step in taking down a brutal dictator and liberating France.

TIMELINE

1 SEPTEMBER 1939: Germany invades Poland, starting World War II.

3 SEPTEMBER 1939: Britain and France declare war on Germany.

10 MAY 1940: Winston Churchill becomes Britain's prime minister.

JUNE 1941: Germany invades the Soviet Union, creating the Eastern Front.

7 DECEMBER 1941: Japan attacks Pearl Harbor, Hawaii, forcing the United States to consider entering World War II.

8 DECEMBER 1941: The United States officially enters World War II.

JUNE 1942: General Dwight D. Eisenhower arrives in London to command US troops that will fight in Europe and North Africa.

4 JUNE 1944: Eisenhower calls off the invasion of Normandy, France, that had been scheduled for 5 June.

5 JUNE 1944: Eisenhower chooses 6 June as D-Day for the Normandy invasion.

6 JUNE 1944:

12.00 A.M.: Allied glider planes begin landing in Normandy. They are followed by thousands of paratroopers.

4.00 A.M.: Allied troops begin boarding the landing craft that will take them ashore.

5.00 A.M.: As dawn comes, German soldiers on the beaches begin spotting the Allied naval force in the English Channel.

APPROXIMATELY 5.30 A.M.: Allied ships off the coast begin to bombard German positions on the shore.

6.30 A.M.: The first American troops come ashore at Omaha and Utah beaches.

7.25 A.M.: British and Canadian forces begin coming ashore at their three assigned beaches.

9.33 A.M.: An aide to General Eisenhower announces the news of the Normandy invasion.

7 June 1944: Eisenhower visits the Normandy beaches on the ship *Apollo*.

27 June 1944: American forces capture the port of Cherbourg.

15 August 1944: The Allies launch Operation Dragoon in southern France.

25 August 1944: The Allies retake Paris.

16 December 1944: The Germans launch their last major offensive at the Battle of the Bulge but cannot stop the advancing Allied forces.

7 May 1945: Germany surrenders, ending the war in Europe.

14 August 1945: Japan's unconditional surrender to the Allies is announced, effectively ending World War II.

GLOSSARY

Allies group of countries that fought together in World War II; some of the Allies were Great Britain, the United States, Canada and France

amphibious military action involving forces landing and attacking from the sea

artillery large guns, such as missile launchers, that require several soldiers to load, aim and fire

atrocity act that is usually considered monstrous by most societies

bunker underground shelter from bomb attacks and gunfire

casualty someone who is injured, captured, killed or missing in an accident, a disaster or a war

front area where two armies are fighting

intelligence secret information about an enemy's plans or actions

meteorologist person who studies and predicts the weather

mortar short cannon that fires shells or rockets high in the air

paratrooper soldier trained to jump by parachute into battle

reinforcements extra troops sent into battle

Soviet Union former group of 15 republics that included Russia, Ukraine and other nations in eastern Europe and northern Asia

tracer ammunition that leaves a colourful trail to help a shooter determine if an intended target is being hit

COMPREHENSION QUESTIONS

1. Why did General Eisenhower want to launch D-Day between 4 June and 7 June?

2. Describe how conditions for the Americans at Utah Beach differed from what they found at Omaha Beach. Support your answer using information from at least two other texts or valid Internet sources.

3. How did the people of France react to the landing of the Allies and why? How did they react to the damage caused to French villages? Support your answer using information from at least two other texts or valid Internet sources.

FIND OUT MORE

BOOKS

Battles of World War II, Neil Tonge (Wayland, 2013)

D-Day, Henry Brook (Usborne, 2014)

D-Day: 6 June 1944, Agnieszka Biskup (Raintree, 2014)

World War II: Visual Encyclopedia (DK Children, 2015)

WEBSITES

www.bbc.co.uk/education/guides/z9s9q6f/revision

This website provides a summary of what happened during the war.

www.dkfindout.com/uk/history/world-war-ii

Find out more about World War II on this website.

news.bbc.co.uk/cbbcnews/hi/find_out/guides/world/d-day_/
newsid_3754000/3754731.stm

This website gives more details about D-Day.

SELECTED BIBLIOGRAPHY

Air War D-Day: Gold Juno Sword. Vol. 5, Martin Bowman (Pen & Sword Aviation, 2013)

Band of Brothers: E Company, 506th Regiment, 101st Airborne from Normandy to Hitler's Eagle's Nest, Stephen Ambrose (Simon & Schuster, 2001)

Beyond Band of Brothers: The War Memoirs of Major Dick Winters, Richard D. Winters (Berkley Caliber, 2006)

Crusade in Europe, Dwight D. Eisenhower (Johns Hopkins University Press, 1997)

D-Day as They Saw It, Jon E. Lewis, ed (Carroll & Graf, 2004)

D-Day: Minute by Minute, Jonathan Mayo (Marble Arch Press, 2014)

D-Day Through French Eyes: Normandy 1944, Mary Louise Roberts (The University of Chicago Press, 2014)

Grenadiers: The Story of Waffen SS General Kurt "Panzer" Meyer, Kurt Meyer (Stackpole Books, 2005)

Ike: An American Hero, Michael Korda (Harper, 2007)

The Germans in Normandy, Richard Hargreaves (Stackpole Books, 2008)

Three Years with Eisenhower: The Personal Diary of Captain Harry C. Butcher, USNR, Naval Aide to General Eisenhower, 1942 to 1945, Harry C. Butcher (W. Heinemann Ltd., 1946)

Voices of D-Day: The Story of the Allied Invasion, Told by Those Who Were There, Ronald J. Drez, ed (Louisiana State University Press, 1994)

INDEX

ABOUT THE AUTHOR

Michael Burgan is a freelance writer who specializes in books for children and young adults, both fiction and non-fiction. A graduate of the University of Connecticut in the United States with a degree in history, Burgan is also a produced playwright and the editor of *The Biographer's Craft*, the newsletter for Biographers International Organization. He lives in New Mexico, USA.